Junior Drug Awareness

Prozac
& Other
Antidepressants

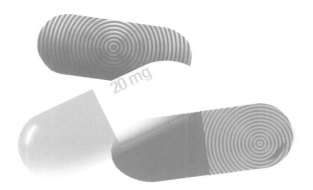

Junior Drug Awareness

Alcohol

Amphetamines and Other Uppers

Crack and Cocaine

Ecstasy and Other Designer Drugs

Heroin

How to Get Help

How to Say No

Inhalants and Solvents

LSD, PCP, and Other Hallucinogens

Marijuana

Nicotine and Cigarettes

Pain Relievers, Diet Pills, and
Other Over-the-Counter Drugs

Prozac and Other Antidepressants

Steroids

Valium and Other Downers

Junior Drug Awareness

Prozac
& Other
Antidepressants

Introduction by **BARRY R. McCAFFREY**
Director, Office of National Drug Control Policy

Foreword by **STEVEN L. JAFFE, M.D.**
Senior Consulting Editor,
Professor of Child and Adolescent Psychiatry, Emory University

Stephen Bird

B. Joan McClure, B.N.Sc., R.N.

Chelsea House Publishers
Philadelphia

CHELSEA HOUSE PUBLISHERS
Editor in Chief Stephen Reginald
Production Manager Pamela Loos
Director of Photography Judy L. Hasday
Art Director Sara Davis
Managing Editor James D. Gallagher
Senior Production Editor LeeAnne Gelletly

Staff for PROZAC AND OTHER ANTIDEPRESSANTS
Project Editor Therese De Angelis
Contributing Editor John Ziff
Associate Art Director Takeshi Takahashi
Picture Researcher Sandy Jones
Designer 21st Century Publishing and Communications, Inc.
Cover Illustrator Takeshi Takahashi

Cover Photo © PhotoDisc Vol.45 #45133

The Chelsea House World Wide Web address is
http://www.chelseahouse.com

3 5 7 9 8 6 4 2

Library of Congress Cataloging-in-Publication Data
Bird, Stephen.
Prozac and other antidepressants/Stephen Bird, B. Joan
McClure; introduction by Barry R. McCaffrey, Stephen
L. Jaffe.
    pp.   cm. — (Junior drug awareness series)
Includes bibliographical references and index.
Summary: Describes the symptoms of mental depression
and the effects of Prozac and other antidepressants,
which are used to treat this condition.
ISBN 0-7910-5204-4 (hc)
1. Depression, Mental—Chemotherapy—Juvenile literature.
2. Depression in children—Treatment—Juvenile literature.
3. Fluoxetine—Juvenile literature. 4. Antidepressants—
Juvenile literature. [1. Depression, Mental. 2. Antidepressants. 3. Fluoxetine.] I. McClure, B. Joan. II. Title. III.
Series.
RC537.B4998   1999
616.85'27061—dc21   99–13185
                                                      CIP

CONTENTS

by **Barry R. McCaffrey**
Director, Office of National
Drug Control Policy

STAYING AWAY FROM ILLEGAL DRUGS, TOBACCO PRODUCTS, AND ALCOHOL

G ood health allows you to be as strong, happy, smart, and skillful as you can possibly be. The worst thing about illegal drugs is that they damage people from the inside. Our bodies and minds are wonderful, complicated systems that run like finely tuned machines when we take care of ourselves.

Doctors prescribe legal drugs, called medicines, to heal us when we become sick, but dangerous chemicals that are not recommended by doctors, nurses, or pharmacists are called illegal drugs. These drugs cannot be bought in stores because they harm different organs of the body, causing illness or even death. Illegal drugs, such as marijuana, cocaine or "crack," heroin, methamphetamine ("meth"), and other dangerous substances are against the law because they affect our ability to think, work, play, sleep, or eat.

If anyone ever offers you illegal drugs or any kind of pills, liquids, substances to smoke, or shots to inject into your body, tell them you're not interested. You should report drug pushers—people who distribute these poisons—to parents, teachers, police, coaches, clergy, or other adults whom you trust.

Cigarettes and alcohol are also illegal for youngsters. Tobacco products and drinks like wine, beer, and liquor are particularly harmful for children and teenagers because their bodies, especially their nervous systems, are still developing. For this reason, young people are more likely to be hurt by illicit drugs—including cigarettes and alcohol. These two products kill more people—from cancer, and automobile accidents caused by intoxicated drivers—than all other drugs combined. We say about drug use: "Users are losers." Be a winner and stay away from illegal drugs, tobacco products, and alcoholic beverages.

Here are four reasons why you shouldn't use illegal drugs:

- Illegal drugs can cause brain damage.
- Illegal drugs are "psychoactive." This means that they change your personality or the way you feel. They also impair your judgment. While under the influence of drugs, you are more likely to endanger your life or someone else's. You will also be less able to protect yourself from danger.
- Many illegal drugs are addictive, which means that once a person starts taking them, stopping is extremely difficult. An addict's body craves the drug and becomes dependent upon it. The illegal drug–user may become sick if the drug is discontinued and so may become a slave to drugs.

- Some drugs, called "gateway" substances, can lead a person to take more-dangerous drugs. For example, a 12-year-old who smokes marijuana is 79 times more likely to have an addiction problem later in life than a child who never tries marijuana.

Here are some reasons why you shouldn't drink alcoholic beverages, including beer and wine coolers:

- Alcohol is the second leading cause of death in our country. More than 100,000 people die every year because of drinking.
- Adolescents are twice as likely as adults to be involved in fatal alcohol-related car crashes.
- Half of all assaults against girls or women involve alcohol.
- Drinking is illegal if you are under the age of 21. You could be arrested for this crime.

Here are three reasons why you shouldn't smoke cigarettes:

- Nicotine is highly addictive. Once you start smoking, it is very hard to stop, and smoking cigarettes causes lung cancer and other diseases. Tobacco- and nicotine-related diseases kill more than 400,000 people every year.
- Each day, 3,000 kids begin smoking. One-third of these youngsters will probably have their lives shortened because of tobacco use.
- Children who smoke cigarettes are almost six times more likely to use other illegal drugs than kids who don't smoke.

If your parents haven't told you how they feel about the dangers of illegal drugs, ask them. One of every 10 kids aged 12 to 17 is using illegal drugs. They do not understand the risks they are taking with their health and their lives. However, the vast majority of young people in America are smart enough to figure out that drugs, cigarettes, and alcohol could rob them of their future. Be your body's best friend: guard your mental and physical health by staying away from drugs.

WHY SHOULD I LEARN ABOUT DRUGS?

Steven L. Jaffe, M.D., Senior Consulting Editor,
Professor of Child and Adolescent Psychiatry,
Emory University

Your grandparents and great-grandparents did not think much about "drug awareness." That's because drugs, to most of them, simply meant "medicine."

Of the three types of drugs, medicine is the good type. Medicines such as penicillin and aspirin promote healing and help sick people get better.

Another type of drug is obviously bad for you because it is poison. Then there are the kinds of drugs that fool you, such as marijuana and LSD. They make you feel good, but they harm your body and brain.

Our great crisis today is that this third category of drugs has become widely abused. Drugs of abuse are everywhere, not just in rough neighborhoods. Many teens are introduced to drugs by older brothers, sisters, friends, or even friends' parents. Some people may use only a little bit of a drug, but others who inherited a tendency to become addicted may move on to using drugs all the time. If a family member is or was an alcoholic or an addict, a young person is at greater risk of becoming one.

Drug abuse can weaken us physically. Worse, it can cause

permanent mental damage. Our brain is the most important part of our body. Our thoughts, hopes, wishes, feelings, and memories are located there, within 100 billion nerve cells. Alcohol and drugs that are abused will harm—and even destroy—these cells. During the teen years, your brain continues to develop and grow, but drugs and alcohol can impair this growth.

I treat all types of teenagers at my hospital programs and in my office. Many suffer from depression or anxiety. A lot of them abuse drugs and alcohol, and this makes their depression or fears worse. I have celebrated birthdays and high school graduations with many of my patients. But I have also been to sad funerals for others who have died from problems with drug abuse.

Doctors understand more about drugs today than ever before. We've learned that some substances (even some foods) that we once thought were harmless can actually cause health problems. And for some people, medicines that help relieve one symptom might cause problems in other ways. This is because each person's body chemistry and immune system are different.

For all of these reasons, drug awareness is important for everyone. We need to learn which drugs to avoid or question—not only the destructive, illegal drugs we hear so much about in the news, but also ordinary medicines we buy at the supermarket or pharmacy. We need to understand that even "good" drugs can hurt us if they are not used correctly. We also need accurate scientific knowledge, not just rumors we hear from other teens.

Drug awareness enables you to make good decisions. It allows you to become powerful and strong and have a meaningful life!

Everyone feels blue or downhearted at times. But if these feelings are accompanied by a sense of hopelessness or a loss of interest in your usual activities, you may be suffering from major depression. Read this chapter for other signs that you may be depressed.

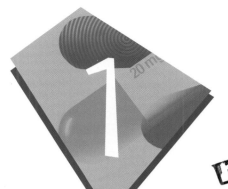

WHAT IS DEPRESSION?

W e use the word "depression" in different ways. Most often, we use it when we feel sad or disappointed about something. For example, you might say, "My parents won't let me go to the park. I'm so depressed." Or, "I'm depressed because I didn't do well on my math test." In both of these cases, depression refers to a short time of feeling "down" or blue.

To a doctor or **psychiatrist,** however, depression refers to a severe psychiatric illness that lasts a long time. This type of depression is called major depressive disorder. A milder, **chronic** form of depression is called **dysthymic disorder**. This term refers to a condition in which one feels mildly depressed over a period of several years. Dr. William S. Appleton, a psychiatrist who teaches at Harvard Medical School, explains what this means in his book *Prozac and the New Antidepressants*: "A depressed mood is a constant sad, dejected feeling lasting at least two weeks, which [is different] from normal blues or discouragement. Although the difference between feeling sad and depression can be hard to distinguish in words, those that have experienced both have little difficulty in telling them apart." Sometimes it takes a long time for a person to overcome depression. Although some people may have to spend time in a hospital or treatment center to get better, most people who suffer from major depressive disorder or dysthymic disorder are treated in a psychiatrist's or medical doctor's office.

Depression has troubled people of all cultures and regions of the world throughout history. But the illness, in its various forms, has remained a mystery. It was only about 30 years ago that doctors began to learn more about depression. Since then, they have also learned that depression can affect people of all ages, including children.

Depression is nobody's fault! Doctors know that there is a strong link between the mind and body. Depression may be caused by a mix of events and conditions, including chemical imbalance, loss, disappointment, unhappy or unstable family life, and an inherited or genetic **predisposition** (a tendency toward a particular action, behavior, or thing). If childhood depression is not recognized and treated, the youngster might grow up to be a depressed adult.

It's difficult to recognize depression in oneself. One

study reports that 12 million people in the United States and 1.2 million people in Canada suffer from depression but don't know it. Depression can be life-threatening: left untreated, it can become so serious that it leads to suicide. About 70 percent of all suicides are the result of untreated major depression.

Signs of Depression

There are many signs and symptoms of major depression, and even healthy people can experience them. Everyone has an occasional "down" day, when they feel blue. But when the feelings continue for a long time and interfere with relationships with family and friends, school work, and normal life, you may be suffering from major depression and should see a doctor.

How can you tell whether a friend or family member suffers from depression? Here are some signs to look for:

- Feels sad or "empty" most of the time
- Does not enjoy things that once brought pleasure
- Feels tired or "slowed down" and speaks slowly
- Has sleep problems (sleeps too often or not enough)
- Overeats or loses appetite
- Feels guilty or worthless for no apparent reason
- Thinks of death or of attempting suicide
- Cries frequently or for no apparent reason
- Feels irritable
- Experiences aches and pains that don't go away

Some people who are depressed seem angry and irritable instead of sad. Kids who suffer from depression may frequently get into trouble at home or school.

- Feels like time is passing very slowly
- Has trouble making decisions
- Has trouble concentrating
- Paces, fidgets, wrings hands, or feels restless

Signs of Childhood Depression

Childhood depression was first recognized about 30 years ago, when doctors noticed that children who were hospitalized or those who suffered chronic or serious illnesses often showed the same symptoms as those seen in depressed adults. To determine whether a child is depressed, doctors ask special questions and look for certain signs, after which they can reliably test and diagnose the child. Sometimes, though, the signs change from week to week or day to day.

Because they feel so low, children who are depressed have trouble concentrating. They often demonstrate learning and attention problems, especially at school. They may take a long time to complete a task, and the quality of their projects may be poor. Their desks and work areas may be messy. They often forget instructions and homework, are not prepared for tests, or they may frequently miss the school bus. They may also fall behind in their schoolwork.

Depressed children may say they don't feel well, or they might complain of headaches or stomachaches. At school, they often visit the nurse and may miss a lot of classwork. At home, they may have trouble concentrating or paying attention to chores, and they need constant guidance and reminders to get things done. Their rooms are usually messy. Children who feel depressed don't have much energy; they might do little but watch TV or daydream.

Children with depression can also exhibit symptoms

of anger or aggression, such as running away from home, lying, stealing, cheating, and talking back. At school, depressed kids may disrupt the classroom by making noises, throwing things, or asking inappropriate questions. They may even fight with or tease other children, and they do not seem to care about the

Nicholas Dubuque poses with his mother, Susan, in the library of his school in Richmond, Virginia. At 10 years old, Nicholas was diagnosed with major depression. After Nicholas seeing a psychiatrist and began to take Prozac, his condition improved. With his mother's help, he wrote a book called *Kid Power Tactics for Dealing with Depression,* which was published in March 1996.

consequences of their behavior. They are easily frustrated, and they react quickly in an angry way, both verbally and physically. When depression shows itself in these ways, it is called masked depression. In other words, the depressed feelings are hidden or "masked" by feelings of anger and behavioral problems. Children who are not diagnosed with masked depression may be labeled as delinquents because of their aggressive behavior.

As we have seen, depression is not new, and it is a common disorder. In what ways have people treated it throughout history? Are there modern ways of curing depression without taking drugs like Prozac? What do Prozac and other **antidepressant** drugs do to you, anyway? We'll find the answers to these questions in the next few chapters.

A Babylonian priest and a physician exorcise demons from a patient. Many ancient cultures believed that a person with depression was possessed by evil spirits.

A HISTORY OF ANTIDEPRESSANTS

I n biblical times, if you suffered from severe depression you might have been said to be possessed by demons. Until the early 1900s, most people believed that those with depression and similar mental conditions were dangerous. Many times, such people were locked away and kept from other people, where their conditions only worsened.

When doctors did attempt to treat people who suffered from depression, the methods were bizarre, difficult, and mostly unsuccessful. For example, in 1812, some depressed people were placed in a new invention called a "gyration device." The patient was strapped into a chair and then spun around at great speed in the hope of sending more blood to the patient's brain and healing him or her. Static electricity (electrotherapy) and water treatments (hydrotherapy) were also used to treat mental illness in the 1800s. Later, doctors added such water therapies as placing patients in steam baths or showers and wrapping them in hot, wet sacks. Although these treatments weren't harmful or painful, they didn't cure depression.

By the late 1800s and early 1900s, mental illness was believed to be the result of nervous exhaustion. An adult who was suffering from depression was described as having had a "nervous breakdown" and was considered mentally and physically frail. As a result, doctors tried to treat depression with what was called the "rest cure." In this type of therapy, patients were isolated from their families and kept in a quiet setting. They were fed well in an effort to "strengthen" their blood and build fat. A patient undergoing the rest cure might also receive frequent massages.

From this treatment another cure called sleep therapy was developed. As the name suggests, sleep therapy patients were kept asleep with drugs such as **barbiturates** and **opium** for up to two weeks. Physicians believed that a long period of sleep would restore the patient's exhausted nervous system. A variation of this treatment was called sleep deprivation therapy, in which a patient was kept awake for about four days at a time and not permitted to fall asleep.

In the 1930s and 1940s, some doctors also treated their depressed patients by exposing them to extreme heat or cold in the hope that they could shock the patients' systems into functioning normally. Patients would be subjected to repeated steaming hot or

Erica Robinson (on the floor, left) visits a mental health specialist with her parents (right) and her sister (on Erica's left) at the West End Health Center in Cincinnati, Ohio. A good program for recovery from depression includes psychotherapy, during which patients are free to share their private thoughts and emotions with a trained mental health professional.

icy baths, for example, or they would be wrapped in cloth that had been immersed in hot or cold water. Sometimes physicians would even perform surgical procedures on patients who were depressed. However, like hot and cold treatments and sleep deprivation, performing surgery to "cure" depression was soon dismissed as ineffective.

During the 1930s and 1940s, doctors also treated

(continued on p. 26)

You're Not Alone

Depression can strike anyone, regardless of age, race, gender, or way of life. Here is a list of some famous people who have struggled with depression:

Buzz Aldrin, *astronaut*

Roseanne Barr, *actress and comedian*

Barbara Bush, *former First Lady*

Drew Carey, *actor and comedian*

Dick Cavett, *author and former talk-show host*

Ray Charles, *musician*

Winston Churchill (1874–1965), *British prime minister*

Dick Clark, *TV personality*

Kurt Cobain (1967–1994), *musician*

Ty Cobb (1886–1961), *baseball player*

Calvin Coolidge (1872–1933), *U.S. president*

Francis Ford Coppola, *film director*

Sheryl Crow, *musician*

Patty Duke, *actress*

James Farmer, *civil rights activist*

Judy Garland (1922–1969), *singer and actress*

Stephen Hawking, *physicist*

Ernest Hemingway (1898–1961), *author*

Margeaux Hemingway (1955–1996), *actress*

John Lennon (1940–1980), *musician*

Abraham Lincoln (1809–1865), *U.S. president*

Jack London (1876–1916), *author*

Sarah McLachlan, *musician*

Alma Powell, the wife of retired U.S. general Colin Powell, has publicly acknowledged her battle with depression. General Powell declined to run in the 1996 presidential election because he was concerned that the added pressure of campaigning might affect his wife's health.

Michelangelo Buonarroti (1475–1564), *artist*

Marilyn Monroe (1926–1962), *actress and singer*

George S. Patton (1885–1945), *U.S. general*

Cole Porter (1891–1964), *composer*

Bonnie Raitt, *musician*

Joan Rivers, *comedian and talk-show host*

Diana Spencer (1961–1997), *Princess of Wales*

James Taylor, *musician*

Vincent Van Gogh (1853–1890), *artist*

Mike Wallace, *news anchor*

Tammy Wynette (1942–1998), *singer and musician*

(continued from p. 23)

depression with drugs that caused seizures or convulsions, like camphor and metrazol. The doctor who first tried this treatment claimed that he had a patient who hadn't moved from bed in four years, but after having five drug-induced seizures, he got up, dressed, and began to show an interest in life again.

This treatment led to the idea of creating seizures through electric shock. This form of treatment was at its peak in the United States in 1935. Unfortunately, people suffered broken bones and dislocated limbs from the violent shaking resulting from the seizures. It was then discovered that a drug called curare could keep the body still and confine the seizure to the brain, making shock treatment easier on the patient.

Electric shock treatment has greatly improved and is still being used for depression. Today, it is known as electroconvulsive therapy or ECT, and it is used only for rare cases in which all other methods of treatment have failed. Despite what many believe, ECT does not cause brain damage, and the procedure is now very safe. Before a treatment session, the patient is given an anesthetic (a drug that causes loss of feeling or consciousness) and is put to sleep. The person also receives oxygen and a muscle-relaxing drug. Scientists are not exactly sure why ECT works, but it has been used successfully in cases of severe depression.

Modern Treatments for Depression

Although sleep deprivation and ECT are still used to some extent with the seriously depressed, today most adults diagnosed with depression are successfully treated with drugs known as antidepressants. Most of these patients, especially those who are diagnosed early in their illness, never have to be in a hospital at all. While the first antidepressant drugs, which were introduced in the 1950s, had many bothersome and uncomfortable side effects, the newest antidepressants have fewer side effects than ever, and sometimes they have none at all. Prozac is one of these newer drugs. We will discuss Prozac and other antidepressants in Chapter 3.

Today, counseling such as **psychotherapy** is usually included along with antidepressant medication to treat depression. Psychotherapy allows you to share your most private thoughts and feelings with an understanding and objective mental health professional, knowing that whatever is said will be kept private. This kind of treatment is most effective when the patient trusts his or her therapist. In some cases, people who get this kind of counseling find that they are able to combat their depression without taking antidepressants at all. We will discuss psychotherapy more fully in Chapter 4.

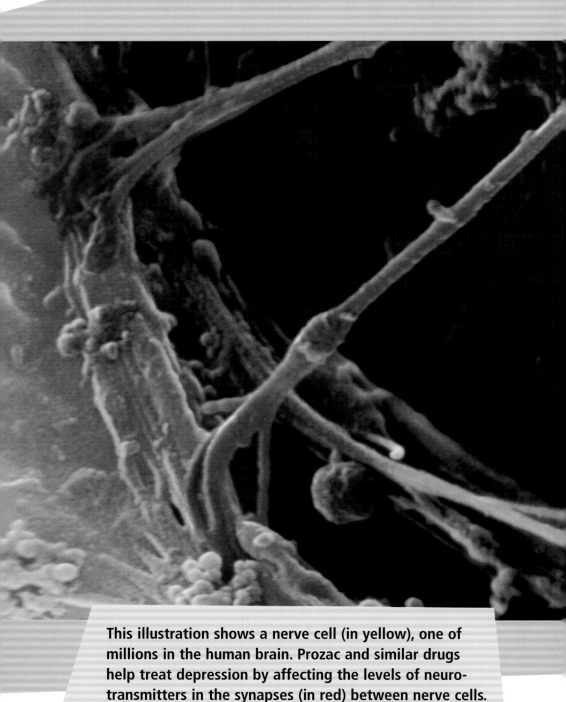

This illustration shows a nerve cell (in yellow), one of millions in the human brain. Prozac and similar drugs help treat depression by affecting the levels of neurotransmitters in the synapses (in red) between nerve cells.

3

HOW ANTIDEPRESSANTS WORK

There is a strong connection between the human mind and the body. Today it is thought that depression may be caused by a combination of factors: a chemical imbalance in the brain, emotional difficulties such as disappointment and loss, family troubles, and inherited (or genetic) factors. We don't know exactly why this mix of factors might lead to depression in one person while it doesn't do so in another. We do know that certain **biochemical** changes take place in a depressed person, but we aren't sure which comes first, the biochemical changes or the depression.

How Do Antidepressant Drugs Help Treat Depression?

Our brains work like computers, constantly sending out thousands of messages, even when we are asleep. These messages are sent by way of chemicals called

neurotransmitters. Some researchers think that an imbalance or malfunction of neurotransmitters can result in depression. However, other medical experts think that the process could occur in the reverse—that depression causes these chemical changes. What we do know is that antidepressants help restore the proper balance of neurotransmitters in the brain.

More than 50 neurotransmitters have been identified in the human brain. A neurotransmitter known as **serotonin** is one of the main chemicals that regulate our moods. Most antidepressant medications work by affecting serotonin levels primarily. Other neurotransmitters, like **dopamine** and **norepinephrine**, have also been studied for their effects on depression.

All antidepressants are prescription drugs. Just like many other products, all prescription drugs have two names: a **trade name** and a **generic name.** For example, Kleenex is a trade name for the generic product facial tissues; another example is Jello, which is a trade name for flavored gelatin. Prozac is a trade name for the generic drug **fluoxetine**.

Antidepressants don't work as quickly as many of the other medicines we take for relief of aches and pains. Instead, even though antidepressants are taken daily, they can take up to six weeks to become effective. Finding the proper antidepressant drug and determining the most effective dose (amount of drug) for a patient is sometimes a matter of trial and error, but it is crucial for the treatment to be successful.

Some people who take antidepressants experience

Unlike drugs such as aspirin, antidepressants do not offer instant relief from depression. It takes several weeks until an antidepressant reaches an effective level in the bloodstream. This is why it is important that people on such medications take the drug every day and do not stop taking it without consulting the doctor who prescribed it.

side effects, although about half the people who take them experience none. Side effects may include symptoms such as dry mouth, nausea, tiredness, and restlessness; side effects can also differ among specific drugs and patients. Often, these unpleasant feelings subside after the patient has been taking the drug for a few weeks.

In the United States, the Food and Drug Administration (FDA) must approve the use of all new drugs, while in Canada drugs are regulated by the Health Protection Branch of Health Canada. So far, no antidepressant drugs have been specifically approved to treat depression in children. However, scientists are conducting many new studies on how certain types of antidepressants can help kids, and some doctors have already begun prescribing these drugs for depressed children.

What Kinds of Antidepressant Drugs Are Available?

In 1951, a drug called iproniazid was being used in the United States to treat tuberculosis. It was noticed that the drug had the added benefit of improving the patients' moods. This drug belongs in a class of drugs called **monoamine oxidase inhibitors** (**MAOIs**). Five years later, a doctor in Switzerland developed a new drug called imipramine (Tofranil), which belongs in another class of drugs called **tricyclic antidepressants** (**TCAs**). After the two classes of drugs were tested, doctors were able to state that both did indeed help improve a person's mood or sense of well-being, and so they were recognized as the first antidepressant medicines. More recently, a third class of antidepressant drugs has been developed. These are called **selective serotonin-reuptake inhibitors** (**SSRIs**). Prozac is the most well-known SSRI. Let's have a look at each of these three classes of drugs, and then examine a few others as well.

Monoamine Oxidase Inhibitors (MAOIs)

As antidepressants, MAOIs work by helping to increase the levels of serotonin, norepinephrine, and dopamine that the brain releases when it needs to send a message. MAOIs do this by interfering with the flow of those three neurotransmitters, thereby keeping more of the neurotransmitters in contact with the receptors (the parts of nerve cells that "receive" the chemicals). Some of the most common MAOIs are phenelzine (Nardil), isocarboxazid (Marplan), and tranylcypromine (Parnate).

MAOIs are often prescribed for people who have certain symptoms that are not common in typical depression. They include extreme anxiety and panic, increased appetite, and a sad mood that may get worse toward evening. While MAOIs are very effective for relieving depression in some people, the drugs can have unpleasant side effects, including sleepiness, headaches, weakness, dry mouth, and constipation. However, these side effects usually disappear after the prescribed medications have been taken for a while.

One common problem with MAOIs is that they can't be taken with foods that contain a substance called tyramine. Tyramine is present in cheese, some deli meats, certain types of fish, figs, yeast, avocadoes, bananas, caffeine (found in many cola drinks), chocolate, and yogurt, and this substance can cause dangerously high blood pressure if taken with MAOIs. Because people like to avoid these limitations and risks,

(continued on p. 36)

Foods and Beverages to Avoid While Taking an MAOI

Although MAOI antidepressants are safe and effective, they can prevent the body from breaking down a substance called tyramine and may thus produce dangerously high blood pressure. For this reason, people on MAOIs must adhere to a restricted diet of foods that do not contain tyramine. Here is a list of some of the foods and beverages one must avoid while taking an MAOI:

- Anchovies
- Avocados, especially when overripe
- Bananas, especially when overripe
- Beans
- Beer and ale
- Cheese, especially sharp or aged
- Chocolate
- Coffee and other drinks containing caffeine
- Deli meats, especially pepperoni and salami
- Figs
- Fish, especially smoked, aged, or dried
- Liver (beef or chicken)
- Pizza
- Raisins
- Sauerkraut
- Sour cream
- Soy sauce
- Wine (including alcohol-free wine)
- Yeast extracts
- Yogurt

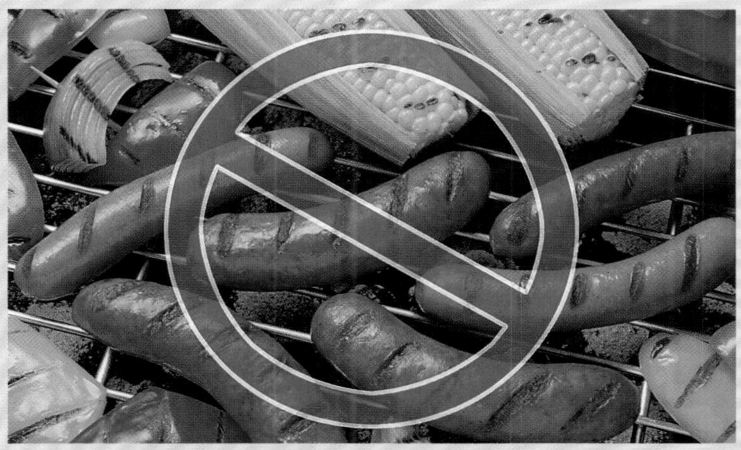

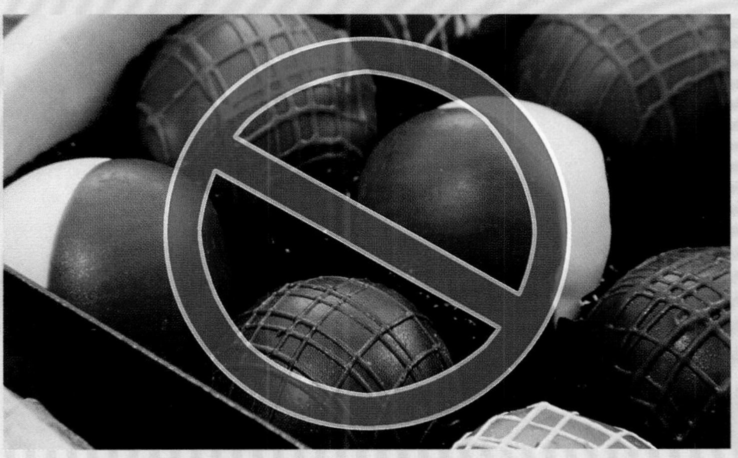

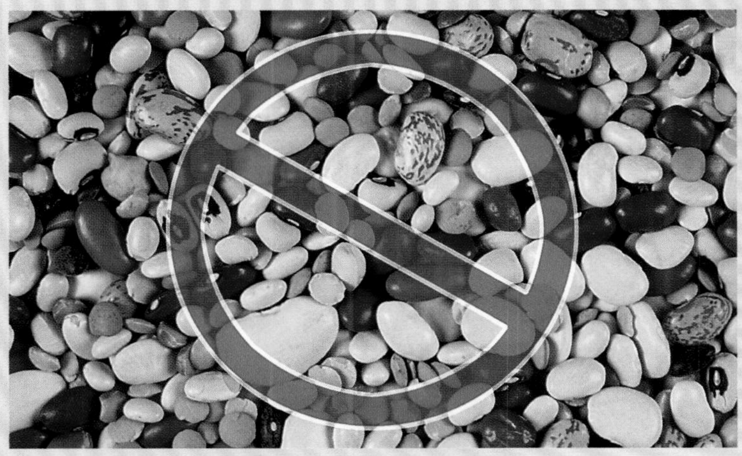

(continued from p. 33)

MAOIs are not as popular with patients and doctors as other antidepressants are. Also, MAOIs must never be taken with SSRIs.

Tricyclic Antidepressants (TCAs)

After the brain has released neurotransmitters to send a message, a "cleanup" of neurotransmitters begins. This is called reuptake. TCAs work by slowing down the chemical "cleanup crew" so that the neuro-transmitters (such as serotonin, norepinephrine, and dopamine) stay effective longer than usual, and the patient feels better for a longer period of time.

TCAs were the first drugs that were widely prescribed for depression, and they are still used today. The main TCAs prescribed to treat depression are imipramine (Tofranil), amitriptyline (Elavil), desipramine (Norpramin), and nortriptyline (Pamelor).

The most common side effects of TCAs are similar to those produced by MAOIs—sleepiness, blurred vision, dry mouth, and constipation. But after a time, the unpleasantness of these side effects usually dimin-ishes. TCAs are not addictive, but if taken in larger doses than prescribed, they can lead to serious physical problems or even cause death.

Some doctors have found that TCAs, especially imipramine, are useful in treating depressed children. But as with MAOIs, the research on children using TCAs is scarce, and the results differ among various studies.

Selective Serotonin-Reuptake Inhibitors (SSRIs)

This is the class of drugs that includes Prozac and similar drugs like Paxil, Zoloft, and Luvox. These new drugs are more effective in treating depression than MAOIs and TCAs because they do not affect all the neurotransmitters. Instead, they are "selective" to serotonin only. Like TCAs, they slow down the reuptake of serotonin, so that more of the chemical is available in the brain.

One of the reasons why Prozac and other SSRIs have become so popular in treating depression is that they cause fewer side effects than other antidepressants do. A few people who take them experience rashes, insomnia, nausea, weight changes, headaches, or anxiety, but these side effects usually subside after a few weeks and do not return.

SSRIs are not addictive. Usually, a person takes an antidepressant drug for six to nine months before his or her doctor gradually decreases the dose. This way, the doctor or psychiatrist prescribing the drug can watch for a recurrence of symptoms or a relapse into depression. A person who has experienced one bout with depression has a 50 percent chance of having symptoms return. A person who has suffered three attacks, has a 90 percent chance of suffering from another bout of depression. These statistics illustrate why doctors sometimes recommend that a patient take SSRIs on an ongoing basis if he or she continues to have episodes of

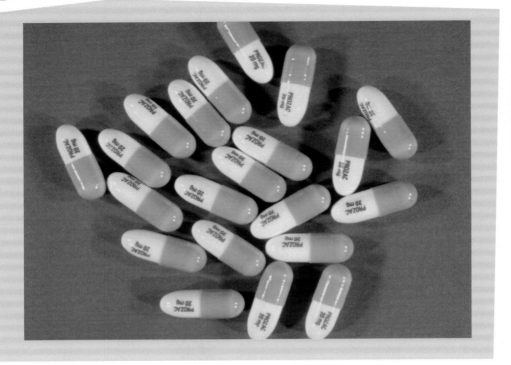

A photograph of 20-milligram Prozac capsules. Prozac is the most widely known of several antidepressants known as selective serotonin-reuptake inhibitors, which work by altering the level of the neurotransmitter serotonin in the brain.

deep depression while off the drug.

Prozac, whose generic name is fluoxetine, first came into use in the United States in 1988. Many people who have used Prozac report that their depression is lifted, they feel more alive and positive, their memory and concentration are improved, and they are less distracted, more thoughtful, and more confident while taking it. In patient after patient, doctors have seen dramatic improvements where other types of antidepressants have failed. Patients taking SSRIs seem not so much "cured" as "transformed." In fact, one patient was so happy with the results of her medication that she reportedly changed her name to Ms. Prozac! Other patients, who say that they had almost forgotten how it felt to be rested and to feel hope, report that with Prozac they feel more relaxed, more energetic, and more comfortable in social situations.

The Risks of SSRIs

Can this much relief come from taking just one pill each day? Some people, including doctors, worry that SSRIs like Prozac are seen as "mood brighteners" that can enhance normal function and increase performance. They report that salespeople and others whose jobs depend upon remaining upbeat misuse SSRIs to gain an edge in a competitive marketplace. But SSRIs are serious drugs that should be used only to treat specific mental disorders or illnesses.

Some people who struggle with depression worry that, instead of enhancing one's mood or improving behavior, taking an SSRI may actually change one's personality. Many people taking these drugs, however, believe that the medication has only made them "more like themselves." One woman interviewed by Peter D. Kramer, the author of *Listening to Prozac,* explained the effect of Prozac: "I am myself, but no longer shut out of everything. I am more comfortable in myself—not empty inside."

When Prozac was first introduced, there were reports that it caused severely depressed patients to become preoccupied with suicidal thoughts or that it increased the frequency of suicidal thoughts they were already having. Other disturbing reports suggested that Prozac created violent behavior in some patients. Both of these reports have since been disproved. In fact, one of the effects of SSRIs is to raise the level of serotonin in the brain, and that helps reduce feelings of violence or aggression.

There is also concern about long-term use of SSRIs. Prozac and other SSRIs have been on the market for a relatively short period, so it's difficult to know whether they will cause any long-term problems or side effects in people who use them on an ongoing basis. However, most researchers and physicians believe that the benefits of SSRIs far outweigh any potential long-term risks.

Even though SSRIs have not been officially approved for use in children, some medical doctors and psychiatrists believe that these drugs can greatly benefit depressed children. Some physicians are already prescribing Prozac to their young patients, taking care to monitor them closely for unexpected side effects or problems related to the drug. And new research on the use of SSRIs for children is promising. A 1996 review of treatments for childhood depression found that SSRIs seem to be safe and effective. A 1997 medical study showed encouraging results for children and teens taking SSRIs.

Like all the SSRIs, Prozac must *not* be mixed with MAOIs. When a doctor switches a patient from one type of antidepressant to another, the patient must undergo a four- to six-week period, called a washout period, during which he or she takes no drug at all. This is especially important when switching from an MAOI to an SSRI; a doctor must carefully monitor the patient while he or she makes the transition.

Other Medical Uses for SSRIs

As doctors became more confident about the results of SSRIs, they began to prescribe Prozac and other

Some people fear that Prozac and similar antidepressants change the user's personality rather than simply improve his or her mood. In fact, people taking SSRIs do not get "high" or become different people. Instead, their symptoms of depression become less intense and they are able to function better than they could before taking medication.

Until recently, most people believed that children do not suffer from major depression. As a result, most of the research on antidepressants like Prozac has been conducted only on adults. However, recent studies show that 5 to 10 percent of children and adolescents may experience major depression. New research has begun to measure the effects of antidepressants on youngsters.

SSRIs for conditions other than depression. Research studies have confirmed that SSRIs also help to relieve a number of mental disorders.

The first condition other than depression that doctors treated with SSRIs was **obsessive-compulsive disorder**. Obsessive-compulsive disorder can take many forms. The most commonly seen forms are constant or habitual handwashing and other cleaning routines, and checking and rechecking that electrical appliances and lights are turned off. These behaviors are extreme forms of what most of us experience from time to time. For example, did you ever go out and then think that you forgot to lock the door? Perhaps you've been on your way to school when you suddenly worry that you forgot your homework, only to find that it's in your backpack after all. People with obsessive-compulsive disorder have problems like this to the point where they can't get on with day-to-day living. For example, they can't leave the house because they have to keep returning to check the iron or the stove. Or they may be so fearful of germs that they wash their hands until their skin is raw, clean the house over and over, or even dust coat hangers.

Research has shown that Prozac and another SSRI called Luvox seem to help people who suffer from this disorder. When treated with these drugs, most patients with obsessive-compulsive disorder report great improvement.

Some of the symptoms of depression in children are similar to those of another disorder called **attention deficit hyperactivity disorder** (**ADHD**). People who suffer from ADHD are easily distracted and do things impulsively (with little or no thought beforehand). They are also **hyperactive** (excessively active) and may be very aggressive (quick to attack or start a fight). One study found that about 3.5 million children in the United States suffer from ADHD.

In the 1930s, an American doctor discovered something interesting about **stimulants**—drugs that increase the body's activities. He learned that giving stimulants to children with ADHD seemed to calm them down. Forty years later, one stimulant in particular, called **Ritalin**, had become the most popular medication for treating ADHD. Today, some children with the disorder take an SSRI with Ritalin, and others take an SSRI alone. The drugs help people with ADHD behave less aggressively and become less hyperactive.

Prozac and other SSRIs are also used to treat anxiety and social phobias. Prozac has also been officially approved for treating eating disorders such as anorexia nervosa and **bulimia**.

Other Drugs Used for Depression

In the search for the most effective antidepressant, scientists have developed several other drugs that don't fit precisely into the three groups we have already discussed. These other drugs also work by acting on specific neurotransmitters in the brain. Some of the most popular ones are **bupropion** (**Wellbutrin**), which affects dopamine; **trazodone** (**Desyrel**), which affects serotonin; and **venlafaxine** (**Effexor**), which affects serotonin, norepinephrine, and dopamine.

Another drug, called **lithium**, is prescribed for patients with **bipolar disorder**, which you may know by its former name, manic depression. With bipolar disorder, the patient's moods swing widely from periods of deep depression to periods of extreme excitement, activity, and agitation (known as mania). Treatment with lithium stabilizes these wild swings, making the patient feel more emotionally balanced.

But lithium can build up in the body to poisonous levels, so patients must have their blood tested about once a month as a precaution against this. The main side effects of lithium include thirst, stomach upset, diarrhea, and weight gain.

If you think you're suffering from depression or if you know someone who is, be sure to talk about the problem with your parents or another adult you can trust. Medications such as SSRIs can help many people recover from or manage depression, but they are not always necessary. In Chapters 4 and 5, we'll look at other ways that people can overcome depression and live healthy and happy lives.

Even if you feel depressed, you may not need to take medication. One of the best ways to sort out your feelings is to seek help from a trained counselor or psychotherapist.

PSYCHOTHERAPY

C an you imagine this? You've been feeling sad and downhearted, everything seems dismal, and the future appears hopeless to you. Perhaps you've had some problems at school, or you feel as though you have no friends. Maybe you've lost interest in your usual hobbies and activities, and the computer or the TV has become your best friend. People try to make you feel better, but nothing works. You and your family can't figure out what's wrong with you.

You go to a doctor, maybe even to several doctors, and after a series of tests, you find out that you're not physically sick. Instead, you are suffering from depression.

What is depression? What is wrong with you? Can you be cured? Your doctor tells you and your parents that you should see a psychotherapist. Why do you need that? Who will you see for this treatment? What can you expect when you go there?

What is Psychotherapy?

Psychotherapy is one of the most important ways to treat depression. When a doctor prescribes medicine like Prozac or another antidepressant, he or she usually arranges for some type of psychotherapy or counseling to go with it. Sometimes people who are depressed don't even need medication; psychotherapy alone can often ease depression. Research shows that the best treatment for childhood depression, however, includes both taking an antidepressant medication and undergoing psychotherapy.

Sometimes depression can lead you to behave poorly or disruptively. Psychotherapy can help you sort out your feelings and find new ways to look at difficult situations.

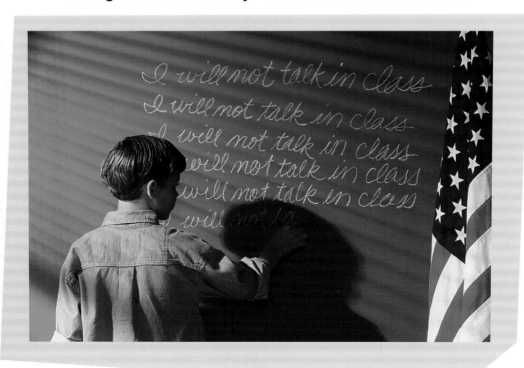

In psychotherapy, you spend time talking to a special kind of doctor about the way you feel. The hope is that once you get your feelings and worries out in the open, you will feel better. Psychotherapy also allows you to talk to someone who will take time to listen, offer support and understanding, and help work out your problems or complicated feelings. Sometimes, if your feelings are too painful to face at all, talking to a trained expert will help you understand what those feelings really are.

Sometimes all that a depressed person needs is to change his or her view of the world and learn how to develop a more positive outlook about difficult or painful situations. The therapist can help you learn to do these things by pointing out new ways to look at certain problems or situations, and by helping you recognize when you are unconsciously thinking in negative ways. For example, maybe you think that your parents are the cause of your troubles. Or you might say, "My teacher hates me. That's why I got in trouble at school." A more accurate view might be that you are behaving differently because you feel depressed, and your parents or teacher are reacting to that change in behavior.

Who Are These Psychotherapists?

Different types of professionals are qualified to be psychotherapists. Sometimes a therapist is the same person who prescribes an antidepressant. This could be a medical doctor who has had some training in how to counsel, but often it is a psychiatrist. A psychiatrist is a professional who first became a medical doctor, then studied mental illnesses such as depression for four more years before earning his or her degree.

Another type of therapist is a **psychologist.** Psychologists are not medical doctors, but they have studied how the mind works and are able to counsel others about what troubles them. Social workers, who have various kinds of training, can also act as therapists at times. Your school probably has a guidance counselor who may be trained to provide therapy as well. Many communities throughout the country also have mental health centers that can provide information about different types of therapists.

No matter what kind of psychotherapist you might see, it's important that you feel comfortable with and trust that person. Having a good relationship with your therapist will help you make positive changes in how you feel. If you do not trust your therapist or you feel that he or she does not understand your problems, don't be afraid to speak up. You may need to try a different kind of therapy or see a different therapist.

How to Get Started

Psychotherapy is not an instant cure for depression. It takes time to get to know your counselor. The first few visits may even seem pointless. The therapist will explain routine matters, such as how often you'll meet. He or she will also talk about keeping what you say confidential. This means that whatever you discuss will be kept private, even from your family members and parents. Therapists generally like to talk to children alone, without their parents. This is because about 70 percent of children will deny the depth of their problems when asked about them in front of their parents. A therapist may, however, start by meeting with your parents to hear their thoughts about how you are behaving or feeling.

You will have to answer a lot of questions that may make you wonder why you're talking to a therapist at all. But this is the quickest way for the therapist to find out exactly how you think and feel. If you are patient and go along with the slow but steady process, you may find yourself looking forward to your appointments because they make you feel better and help you think more clearly. Remember, it's probably the depression that is making you feel that all these questions are pointless.

Many people who undergo psychotherapy also find that as their treatment continues, they begin to learn more about themselves. As a result, they begin thinking of topics they want to discuss during their next session.

What Will Happen in Psychotherapy

The therapist needs to get a picture of you and the world you live in. To do this, he or she will need to ask you lots of questions about your life, including questions about your family members and friends, your hobbies and interests, your likes and dislikes, the neighborhood where you live or grew up, and your pets.

Next, you may be asked about your physical self: how well you sleep, what you eat, whether you have any aches or pains, and whether you've ever been sick or injured. The reason for these questions is that the therapist needs to find out whether the depression is causing or is caused by health problems.

The toughest questions to answer will probably come after you've had a few visits with your therapist. He or she will ask you questions about your emotions. What makes you feel sad or angry? Have you lost anyone who is important to you, perhaps a family member, relative, or friend? What kind of a person do you think you are? Do you feel worthwhile, well liked, or important?

By listening to your answers, the therapist can help you discover why you're feeling depressed and how you can overcome the feelings. For example, the therapist may discover that you don't feel very good about yourself or that you may be angry but unable to figure out why, and so you blame other people for your problems. Maybe someone you loved or trusted has died or moved away, and you need help to get over that grief; maybe you have a hard time making friends and need help finding ways to get along with other people. Perhaps there are even things going on in your life that you find unbearable but don't know how to change.

What Happens Next?

You've now come to the point where the many questions are over. You and your therapist have come to like and respect each other. You trust that what you say does not get passed on to your parents, teachers, or anyone else.

After that part of the therapy process is complete, often your visits will consist of just sitting and talking over feelings, worries, beliefs, and concerns. The office will be a quiet, pleasant place where you feel understood.

Do you have a pet? This may be one of the questions a therapist asks you if you seek help for depression. This kind of information may not seem related to your problem, but asking questions about your life is the best way for a therapist to get to know you and help you feel better.

Therapists can help you to express how you feel inside. They will give you feedback and suggestions and help you regain your self-esteem. They will help you see that you are a worthwhile person. They will help you get over the grief you might feel from having lost someone or something important to you. If you need help in making friends, they will have good ideas about how to do so.

Even when you know what you're feeling, you don't always have the words to express it. Therapists use techniques that can help you find the right words. One way of helping you express your feelings is through art therapy. (We'll explore this more fully in Chapter 5.) Or a therapist may show you a series of pictures and ask you to explain what you think is going on in them. For example, you might be shown a picture of someone running away from a broken window while another child in the picture stands nearby. The therapist might ask what you think is happening in the picture or how you feel if you put yourself in the place of each character. Depending on your experiences or your feelings, you may answer differently than another patient would. This exercise is a good way for a therapist to understand you and to help you understand yourself.

A Family Matter

Another approach to psychotherapy is to include your whole family in the sessions with your therapist. The way your family members interact with one another can affect how you feel about yourself. Sometimes family members are so entangled in a difficult situation that they can't see things clearly. The therapist can act as a sort of referee among family members or as an objective listener who tries to understand everyone's points of view.

One way a therapist might do this is through role-playing. The therapist will describe a typical family situation and assign everyone to "play the part" of someone else in the family. You might pretend to be

Most people who undergo psychotherapy discuss their problems with a counselor privately. However, in some cases it helps to have one or more family members attend sessions with the counselor to work out difficulties that affect each one of them.

An angry face fills a computer screen as a University of Pittsburgh psychologist explains a computer program that helps reveal people's emotional states. This method is especially useful for treating young people, who often have trouble identifying their feelings.

your father, your mother might pretend to be you, and so on. This helps each family member understand how the others feel. It also shows each member how he or she reacts to a situation, and it allows the therapist to suggest ways you can deal with difficult situations by changing your reaction or behavior.

Whatever method your therapist uses, the goal is the same: to help you learn how to deal with the issues that are contributing to your depression.

Family therapy has another goal as well: it helps other members of your family learn how to cope with your depression and find ways to help you recover.

Antidepressants and psychotherapy are the most important tools in the battle to overcome major depressive disorder. But there are other ways you can help yourself feel better again. We'll examine some of these methods in the next chapter.

Taking medication is just one of many things you can do to overcome depression. Read this chapter for other ways to help yourself feel happy and healthy.

ALTERNATIVE THERAPIES

Alternative therapies are ways other than taking antidepressants or undergoing psychotherapy that help you take care of yourself and feel better about yourself if you suffer from depression. Many have been around for thousands of years. Some of these therapies were the only treatments available until the 20th century, when most people came to believe that standard medicines alone could cure illnesses. But in recent decades, as people have begun to learn more about taking responsibility for their own health and nutrition, some of these therapies have become popular again.

These treatments aren't meant to replace modern medicine or psychotherapy and don't require a prescription from a doctor. However, you should always tell your doctor or therapist what you are doing for yourself as you work to recover from depression.

You may have already tried an alternative therapy without even realizing it. Have you ever rubbed your temples to relieve a headache, applied ice to a sore ankle, drunk herbal tea to relax, or put vitamin E on a cut to reduce the chance of getting a scar? If so, you have tried some simple healing methods. If anybody has ever held your hand when you were worried, fed you chicken soup when you were sick, or put a cold cloth on your forehead when you had a fever or headache, you also experienced some natural healing methods. Let's look at a few alternative therapies that some people believe are useful for helping to relieve depression.

Hypericum Perforatum (St. John's Wort)

Hypericum perforatum, also called **St. John's wort**, is a plant with bright yellow-orange flowers whose petals are peppered with black dots. A non-prescription herbal drug of the same name is made from the plant and is believed to alter the level of serotonin in the brain, much like SSRIs do.

In Germany, more than 50 percent of patients suffering from depression, anxiety, and sleep disorders are treated with the herbal drug. Prozac is used for only 2 percent of German patients with these problems. Around 1993, several research studies found that St. John's wort is useful for treating mild to moderate depression. It is believed to be up to 80 percent as effective as antidepressants like Prozac.

Side effects from taking St. John's wort are rare and

A photo of the *Hypericum perforatum* plant, which is commonly known as St. John's wort. Although extracts of this plant are believed to be nearly as effective as antidepressants such as Prozac, it is never a good idea to take a substance like St. John's wort without first consulting a doctor.

mild, with less than 2.5 percent of patients who take it reporting unpleasant feelings. The most common (but still rare) complaint is stomach upset. The herbal drug also seems to cause sensitivity to light in animals, and it may do the same in some people. As a result, anyone who is already sensitive to sunlight should keep this in mind when considering treatment for depression.

Also, it is important to remember that the health effects of St. John's wort have not been fully studied. Very little is known about its long-term side effects. In addition, since St. John's wort products are not strictly regulated the way prescription antidepressants are, their strength and effectiveness may vary from one manufacturer to another, and even from one package to another.

Art Therapy

Art therapy did not become popular until the 1930s, when doctors began to study their patients' art for clues about their illnesses. About the same time, psychotherapists were discovering that by studying art produced by children, they could sometimes determine what emotions the children were feeling. Today, art therapy is frequently used by mental health professionals.

How does art therapy help you overcome depression? Young people, unlike adults, often have trouble expressing their emotions with words. With simple art materials, you may be able to find a way to express how you feel that doesn't involve words. You don't need art experience or special talent to do this, and creating something that is all your own is a satisfying way to express your feelings, dreams, or frustrations.

Although art therapy is used by many health professionals, you don't need to be a doctor to try it yourself. Use paints, colored pencils, modeling clay, markers, crayons, art paper—even a computer program—and let yourself be creative.

Light Therapy

For some people, depression becomes worse during certain seasons of the year. These people have what is called seasonal affective disorder (SAD), sometimes

Therapists sometimes find clues to how young people feel by examining their artwork. Getting involved in a creative project, such as painting, can also help you express your emotions and identify specific problems you may be having.

referred to as the winter blues. People with SAD may overeat, oversleep, gain weight, or exhibit other symptoms of depression during the fall and winter. The people usually feel better during the spring and summer months, when daylight lasts longer. It is believed that the body and brain need a certain amount of light to function properly, and that without enough light people become more susceptible to mental and physical ailments.

An estimated 5 to 10 percent of the population in the middle and northern parts of North America suffer from SAD. Light therapy, also called phototherapy, is a great choice for children with SAD because it doesn't require drugs and it has a high success rate.

If you feel worse during the winter months than in spring and summer, you may feel better if you get outside more often. Get away from your computer or television for a while. Walk your dog, ride your bike, do some yard work or shovel snow, go ice skating or rollerblading—try any activity that gets you out into the sunshine. You'll get some exercise, and you will probably feel better.

Sound and Music Therapy

Music is the most common form of "sound therapy." It includes singing, chanting, listening to music, songwriting, and writing or reading lyrics. Playing or learning a musical instrument can give you a sense of accomplishment. Learning and performing a piece of music can help you build self-esteem and self-discipline.

Professional therapists use this method with their young patients, but it is easy to try music therapy on your own. Dance a little, sing a little, or write out your feelings in song lyrics. Even listening to a favorite CD with your headphones on can sometimes help brighten your mood.

Diet and Nutrition

If you're like most kids, you think about food only when you are hungry or bored, and then you just fill yourself up on whatever is available or tasty. But there

Do you listen to certain songs or types of music when you feel depressed? Does dancing make you feel more relaxed and alert? Do you feel good about yourself after you've mastered a difficult piece of music on your guitar? Then you probably have already used music therapy without realizing it!

is more to eating than grabbing a bag of potato chips or chowing down on a double cheeseburger. What you eat today affects how you look and feel not only right now but also in the years to come. If you are pigging out on junk food regularly, you may already feel out of shape, tired, or moody. If you continue to eat poorly, you can easily grow into an illness-prone, unhealthy-

One of the best ways to stay healthy in mind and body is to eat the right foods. Keeping your body fit helps you get the rest you need and improves your mood.

looking adult.

One of the best things you can do for your mind and body, especially if you suffer from depression, is to eat well and regularly. In 1996, the U.S. Department of Health and Human Services and the Department of Agriculture released a set of dietary guidelines that Americans should follow if they want to stay healthy and reduce their risk of getting certain ailments and diseases. Here is a list of what you should try to eat every day:

- Bread, cereal, rice, and pasta (carbohydrates): 6 to 11 servings

- Fruits (fresh, frozen, canned, dried, or juices): 2 to 4 servings

- Vegetables: 3 to 5 servings

- Meat, poultry, fish, beans, eggs, and nuts (proteins): 2 to 3 servings

- Milk, yogurt, and cheese (dairy products): 2 to 3 servings

- Fats, oils, and sweets: use sparingly

Eating the right foods not only helps your body stay in shape but it also helps you sleep better and think more clearly when you're awake.

Some researchers also believe that minerals such as zinc are important in the diets of people suffering from depression. Zinc is found naturally in fish, turkey, peanuts, pumpkin seeds, mushrooms, soybeans, and liver. You can also take zinc supplements, just as you would take a daily vitamin. Be sure to check with your doctor before taking any diet supplement, however.

People who suffer from depression often have eating problems, such as overeating or undereating, and find that they are gaining or losing weight as a result. If you think you are overeating or undereating because you are depressed, be sure to discuss this with your doctor or a parent.

Keep Relationships Healthy

Throughout your life, the relationships you have with your family and others play a big part in how you feel, and the stronger and healthier your relationships are, the more likely you are to avoid depression. Research studies show that when families have difficulties, there is a greater chance of the children suffering from depression.

You need friends and family who are available in troubled times and with whom you can enjoy fun times. Sometimes, though, you have to be the one to reach out. Invite someone to do something with you. Join a club or a sports team. Good relationships require knowing how to talk, listen, and work out problems. Here are other things that young people say are important to them in relationships: respect, trust, honesty, caring, and kindness, as well as having your own space, having a sense of humor, having similar likes and interests, being accepted the way you are, and having fun together.

It's important to remember that you can't change someone else. You can change only yourself and how you respond to others. Be sure to treat others with the same respect and concern that you expect from them.

On Your Way to Recovery

Now you have learned about depression. You know that some people suffering from depression need to take prescription medicines and participate in counseling,

If you think you suffer from depression, try talking about your feelings to your parents or another adult you trust. Communication can be the first step toward feeling good again.

such as psychotherapy. You've learned about some alternative therapies that you can use to help yourself when you're feeling down.

You also know that if you are depressed, you need not suffer. You can learn more about major depressive disorder and about the drugs that are available to treat it by reading some of the references listed in the bibliography at the end of this book. Or contact the organizations listed in the "Find Out More" section. Being aware of the kinds of treatments available for depression and knowing how you can help yourself are big steps to feeling happy, cheerful, and healthy.

GLOSSARY

antidepressant—any of a number of drugs used to relieve symptoms of depression.

attention deficit hyperactivity disorder (**ADHD**)—a condition in children and adolescents marked by inattention, impulsiveness, and hyperactivity.

barbiturate—a drug that depresses the central nervous system and is generally used to reduce anxiety or induce euphoria.

biochemical—involving chemical reactions in living organisms.

bipolar disorder—formerly called manic depression, a condition in which a person experiences wide mood swings, from deep depression to extreme excitement, activity, and agitation.

bulimia—an eating disorder in which a person engages in regular periods of "bingeing," or eating a large amount of food at once; they then force themselves to vomit the food they have just eaten, a practice called "purging."

bupropion—the generic name for Wellbutrin, a drug used to relieve symptoms of depression. Bupropion is also prescribed for nicotine addiction under the name Zyban.

chronic—lasting over a long period of time or recurring frequently.

Desyrel—the trade name for trazodone. Although it is not classified as an SSRI, trazodone also inhibits the reuptake of serotonin.

dopamine—a neurotransmitter in the brain that is released by neurons in the limbic system, a part of the brain that controls feelings of pleasure.

dysthymic disorder—a depressed mood lasting over a period of two years or more. Dysthymic disorder is a milder form of depression than major depressive disorder.

Effexor—the trade name for venlafaxine, a drug used to relieve symptoms of depression. Effexor has properties of SSRIs, but also inhibits the reuptake of the neurotransmitters norepinephrine and dopamine.

fluoxetine—the generic name for Prozac.

generic name—not having a trademark or brand name.

hyperactive—extremely or excessively active.

***Hypericum perforatum* (St. John's wort)**—a nonprescription herbal drug, made from the plant of the same name, that is believed to alter the level of serotonin in the brain, much as SSRIs do.

lithium—a drug used to treat bipolar disorder.

monoamine oxidase inhibitor (MAOI)—one of a class of antidepressants that increases the levels of serotonin, norepinephrine, and dopamine in the brain.

neurotransmitter—a chemical that is released by neurons and carries messages between them.

norepinephrine—a neurotransmitter that helps prepare the mind and body for emergencies by widening breathing tubes and making the heart beat faster.

obsessive-compulsive disorder—a disorder characterized by extreme or persistent preoccupation with unreasonable ideas or feelings and by uncontrollable impulses to perform certain acts.

opium—a drug made from the milky juice of the poppy plant *Papaver somniferum*. Opium creates a dreamy, pleasant state of drowsiness. It is extremely addictive.

predisposition—a tendency toward a particular action, behavior, or thing. Some people are predisposed (have a predisposition) to developing major depression.

psychiatrist—a medical doctor who treats mental or emotional disorders.

psychologist—a person who specializes in studying the human mind and behavior.

psychotherapy—treatment of a mental or behavioral disorder through regular discussions with a trained therapist, such as a psychologist or psychiatrist.

Ritalin—the brand name of a stimulant that is prescribed to treat the symptoms of attention deficit hyperactivity disorder (ADHD).

selective serotonin-reuptake inhibitor (SSRI)—any of a group of antidepressant drugs that alter the level of serotonin in the brain. SSRIs include Prozac, Paxil, Zoloft, and Luvox.

serotonin—a neurotransmitter involved in the control of mood, aggression, and sexual behavior.

side effect—a secondary and usually adverse effect, as with a drug.

stimulant—a drug that increases the body's activity.

trade name—a name that identifies a specific product and can be used only by the owner of the product. For example, Prozac is the trade name for fluoxetine.

trazodone—the generic name for Desyrel. Although it is not classified as an SSRI, trazodone also inhibits the reuptake of serotonin.

tricyclic antidepressant (TCA)—any of a group of antidepressants that inhibits the reuptake of serotonin, norepinephrine, and a number of other neurotransmitters in the brain. TCAs also have been used to treat other disorders, such as panic attacks and bulimia, but because of their many side effects they are less popular than SSRIs for treating depression.

venlafaxine—the generic name for Effexor, a drug used to relieve symptoms of depression. Venlafaxine has properties of SSRIs, but also inhibits the reuptake of norepinephrine and dopamine.

Wellbutrin—the trade name for bupropion, which is used to relieve symptoms of depression.

BIBLIOGRAPHY

Appleton, William S. *Prozac and the New Antidepressants.* New York: Penguin Books, 1997.

Ayer, Eleanor H. *Everything You Need to Know About Depression.* New York: Rosen Publishing Group, 1997.

Bloomfield, H., M. Nordfors, and P. McWilliams. *Hypericum and Depression.* Los Angeles: Prelude Press, 1996.

Cytryn, Leon, and D. McKnew. *Growing Up Sad: Childhood Depression and Its Treatment.* New York: W. W. Norton & Company, 1996.

Folkers, G., and J. Engelmann. *Taking Charge of My Mind and Body: A Girl's Guide to Outsmarting Alcohol, Drug, Smoking, and Eating Problems.* Minneapolis, MN: Free Spirit Publishing, 1997.

Garland, E. Jane. *Depression Is the Pits, But I'm Getting Better: A Guide for Adolescents.* Washington, DC: Magination Press, 1997.

Helmer, Diana Star. *Let's Talk About Feeling Sad.* Powerkids Press, 1998.

Ingersoll, Barbara, and Sam Goldstein. *Lonely, Sad and Angry.* New York: Doubleday, 1995.

Loueen, Alexander. *Depression and the Body.* New York: Penguin USA, 1993.

Meier, Paul D., and Jan Meier. *Happiness Is a Choice for Teens.* Nashville, TN: Thomas Nelson, 1997.

Monroe, Judy. *Antidepressants.* Springfield, NJ: Enslow Publishers, 1997.

Newman, Susan. *Don't Be S.A.D.: A Teenage Guide to Handling Stress, Anxiety, and Depression.* New York: Julian Messner, 1991.

Sanders, Pete, and Steve Myers. *Depression and Mental Health.* Brookfield, CT: Copper Beech Books, 1998.

Shamoo, T., and P. Patros. *Helping Your Child Cope with Depression and Suicidal Thoughts.* San Francisco: Jossey-Bass, 1990.

Turkington, C., and E. Kaplan. *Making the Prozac Decision: A Guide to Antidepressants.* Los Angeles: Lowell House, 1997.

Wibbelsman, Charles, and Kathy McCoy. *Life Happens: A Teenager's Guide to Friends, Failure, Sexuality, Love, Rejection, Addiction, Peer Pressure, Families, Loss, Depression, Change, and Other Challenges of Living.* New York: Perigee Books, 1996.

FIND OUT MORE ABOUT ANTIDEPRESSANTS AND DEPRESSION

The following list includes agencies, organizations, and websites that provide information about depression and antidepressants such as Prozac. You can also find out where to go for help with depression.

Agencies and Organizations in the United States

American Psychiatric Association (APA)
1400 K Street, N.W.
Washington, DC 20005
202-682-6325
http://www.psych.org

American Psychological Association
750 First Street, N.E.
Washington, DC 20002-4242
202-336-5500

At Health, Inc.
Eastview Professional Building
1370 116th Avenue, N.E., Suite 201
Bellevue, WA 98004-3825
425-451-4399 or 888-ATHEALTH
http://athealth.com
staff@athealth.com

National Alliance for the Mentally Ill (NAMI)
200 North Glebe Road, Suite 1015
Arlington, VA 22201-3754
703-524-7600
NAMI Helpline: 800-950-NAMI
TDD: 703-516-7991
http://www.nami.org

National Depressive and Manic-Depressive Association
730 North Franklin Street, Suite 501
Chicago, IL 60610-3526
800-826-3632 or 312-642-0049
http://www.ndmda.org
myrtis@aol.com

National Institute of Mental Health
5600 Fishers Lane, Room 7C-02
Bethesda, MD 20857-0001
800-443-3675
http://www.nimh.nih.gov/
nimhinfo@nih.gov

National Mental Health Association
1021 Prince Street
Alexandria, VA 22314-2971
703-684-7722
800-969-NMHA

Agencies and Organizations in Canada

Child Welfare League of Canada
613-235-4412
http://www.magi.com/~cwlc
cwlc@magi.com

Ontario Association of Children's Mental Health Centers
416-921-2109
info@oacmhc.org

Websites

Children and Depression
http://members.aol.com/depress/children.htm

Depression.com
http://www.depression.com

Depression Resources List
http://www.execpc.com/~corbeau/

Health Canada Guide to Federal Programs and Services for Children and Youth
http://www.hc-sc.gc.ca/childhood/youth/fedguide.html

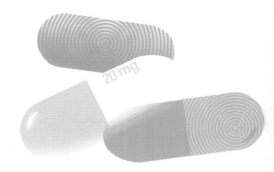

INDEX

Picture Credits

page
6: Courtesy Office of National Drug Control Policy, the White House
12: PhotoDisc #25305
16: Catherine Ursillo/ Photo Researchers, Inc.
18: AP/Wide World Photos
20: Corbis-Bettmann
23: AP/Wide World Photos
25: AP/Wide World Photos
28: Oliver Meckes/ Photo Researchers, Inc.
31: Jeff Greenberg/ Photo Researchers, Inc.
35: Corel Disc 75, #25057
38: Corbis-Bettmann
41: Louise Williams/Science Photo Library/Photo Researchers, Inc.
42: PhotoDisc #45137
46: Ken Lax/Photo Researchers, Inc.
48: PhotoDisc #24170
53: PhotoDisc #24107
55: Stephen Simpson/ FPG International
56: AP/Wide World Photos
58: Richard Hutchings/ Photo Researchers, Inc.
61: Telegraph Colour Library/ FPG International
63: Margaret Miller/ Photo Researchers, Inc.
65: Ron Chapple/ FPG International
66: Ricardo Arias, Latin Stock/ Science Photo Library/ Photo Researchers, Inc.
69: PhotoDisc #24048

STEPHEN BIRD, LL.B., M.A., is a lawyer and author living in Canada.

B. JOAN McCLURE, B.N.Sc., R.N., is the mother of three children, ages 10, 12, and 14.

BARRY R. McCAFFREY is Director of the Office of National Drug Control Policy (ONDCP) at the White House and a member of President Bill Clinton's cabinet. Before taking this job, General McCaffrey was an officer in the U.S. Army. He led the famous "left hook" maneuver of Operation Desert Storm that helped the United States win the Persian Gulf War.

STEVEN L. JAFFE, M.D., received his psychiatry training at Harvard University and the Massachusetts Mental Health Center and his child psychiatry training at Emory University. He has been editor of the *Newsletter of the American Academy of Child and Adolescent Psychiatry* and chairman of the Continuing Education Committee of the Georgia Psychiatric Physicians' Association. Dr. Jaffe is professor of child and adolescent psychiatry at Emory University. He is also clinical professor of psychiatry at Morehouse School of Medicine, and the director of Adolescent Substance Abuse Programs at Charter Peachford Hospital in Atlanta, Georgia.